Las Vegas

TREASURE ISLAND

THE LAS VEGAS STRIP AS IT ACTUALLY APPEARS

(PHOTOGRAPHED IN ONE FRAME.)

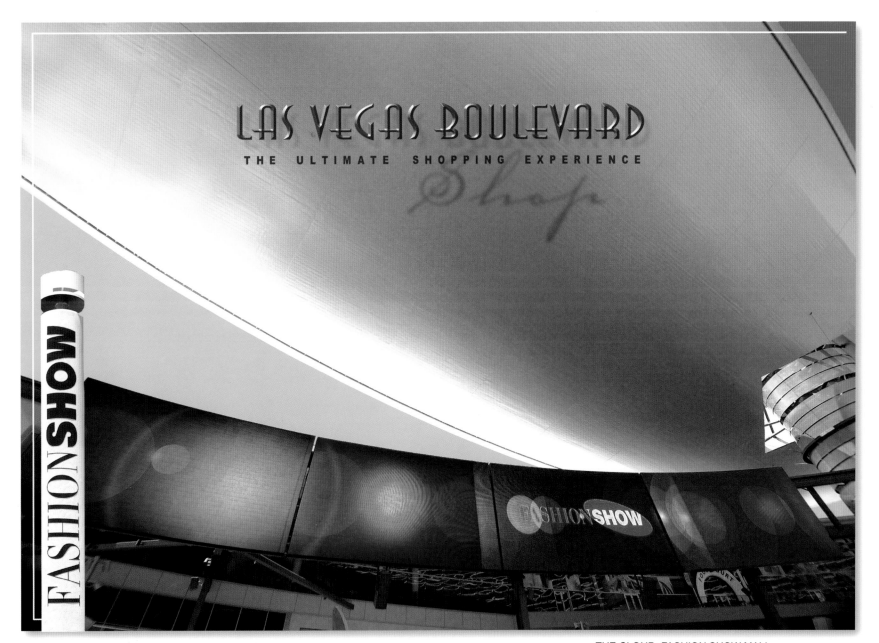

THE CLOUD, FASHION SHOW MALL

CAESARS PALACE

PLANET HOLLYWOOD

CAESARS PALACE
LAS VEGAS

THE COLOSSEUM

CAESARS PALACE

LUXOR LAS VEGAS

Down Town

L A S V E G A S

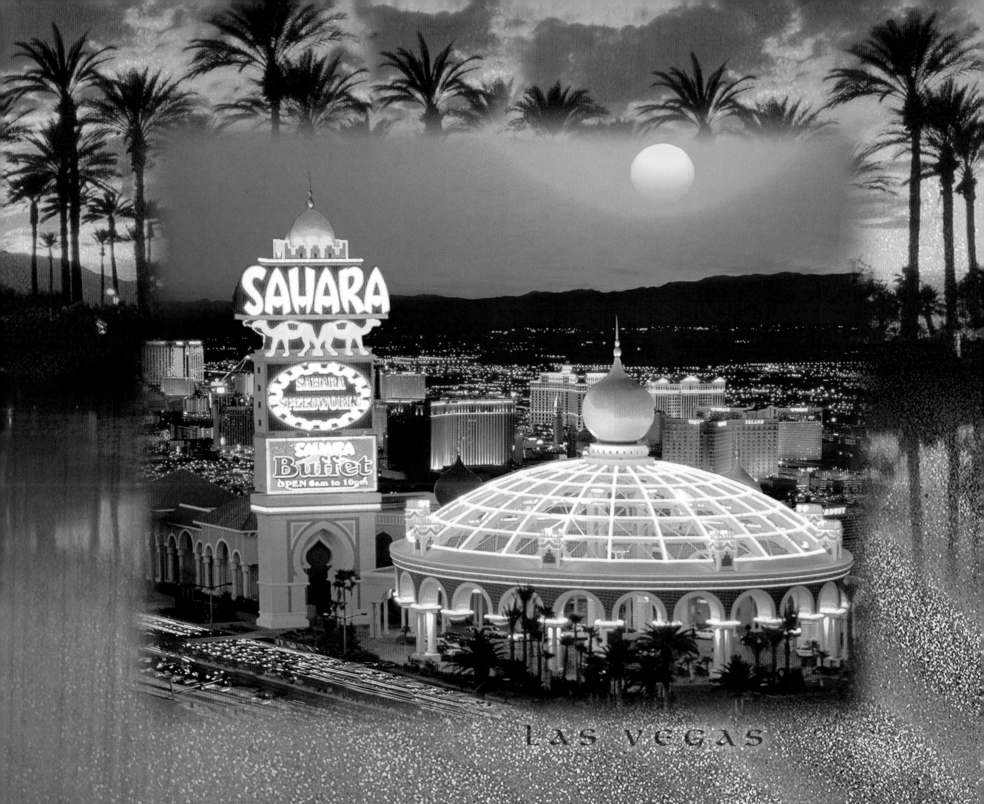

SAHARA

SAHARA SPEEDWORLD

The SAHARA Buffet OPEN 6am to 10pm

las vegas

DEATH VALLEY

Badwater
ELEV. - 282 ft.

RED ROCK CANYON, NEVADA STATE PARK, VISITORS CENTER.

GRAND CANYON

HOOVER DAM

VALLEY OF FIRE

LAKE POWELL

CORKSCREW CANYON

Mesquite
NEVADA

LAUGHLIN

ARCHES

BRYCE CANYON

ARIZONA

ST. GEORGE

ZION

Nevada

THE OTHER SIDE